PHILADELPHIA

IN PHOTOGRAPHS

PHILADELPHIA
IN PHOTOGRAPHS

EDWARD ARTHUR MAUGER

GRAMERCY BOOKS
NEW YORK

INTRODUCTION

Philadelphia is the largest city George Washington ever saw and the only American city he would still recognize. If he stood in front of the Visitor Center at Sixth and Market streets today and surveyed Independence Mall, he would see the elegant State House of Pennsylvania where he reluc-

tantly served as chairman for the Constitutional Convention in 1787. The Marquis de La Fayette, Washington's favorite Frenchman, gave the building its present name, the Hall of Independence.

Next to it, Washington would see Congress Hall, where the House of Representatives demanded to review the secret communiqués behind the first president's unpopular treaty with England. Realizing that his every decision set precedents for his successors, Washington defied the Congress and dared them to impeach him.

To the left of the Statehouse stands Philadelphia's Federal City Hall. The city shared this building with the Supreme Court in the 1790s, much to the justices' relief. During their first year in New York, the Supreme Court had met above a sheep market.

One building George Washington would not be able to find is the rented mansion where he spent seven years inventing the presidency. The remains of the house are interred under a grassy mound, passed over by millions of visitors on their way into the Liberty Bell Pavilion. In fact, the entrance to the great Bell of Liberty rises from the very location where Washington housed his servants and slaves.

A dozen years before Washington governed from his Market Street mansion, his rival, British commander Sir William Howe, occupied that very house. Hoping to quash the American rebellion, Howe's troops had taken the rebel capital. While the Patriot soldiers were encamped twenty-five miles up the Schuylkill River, shivering in Valley Forge, Howe and his officers were raising their glasses by the hearths of the City Tavern.

Philadelphia, now in its fourth century, is full of exquisite ironies and layered with dramatic events. One such irony is the fact that this Revolutionary War capital was originally a pacifist utopia. When English King Charles II gave William Penn a 45,000 square mile colony, making him the world's largest

private real estate developer, he pressed Penn to take a regiment of soldiers for protection "against those savages." The pacifist Quaker objected: "The Indians have been killed and robbed by the settlers. Let us now try what love will do."

When Penn arrived aboard the ship *Welcome* in 1682, the Lenape Indians paddled out to meet this unusual Englishman who had promised to live at peace with them, and to build a "Great Towne, with no wall to keep them out." Unlike other colonial cities, Philadelphia, the city of brotherly love, would not be surrounded by a stockade. The Quaker founder adopted the Roman grid pattern for military cities, with wide straight streets for troop movements, and turned it into a city accessible from every direction. Penn's plan was not just a political statement. He also wanted a city that "would never be burnt and always be wholesome," in contrast to his native London, whose crooked medieval streets had helped to spread the Great Fire in 1666. The same men who rebuilt London migrated to Penn's new capital and erected red brick Georgian homes, and developed America's oldest residential street, Elfreth's Alley. Carpenters Hall presides over the third block of Chestnut Street, a testament both to

Visitor Center: *The best starting point for a tour of Philadelphia is the Visitor Center at Sixth and Market streets. Helpful and well-prepared staff at the concierge counter provide an excellent orientation to guests, including information tailored to their special interests. Orientation films, free maps, free tickets for Independence Hall, light refreshments at the café, and a well-stocked book and souvenir store are featured here, as well as convenient, twenty-four-hour parking in an underground garage.*

Liberty Bell and Independence Hall: *The State House of Pennsylvania—Independence Hall—was Benjamin Franklin's first public business office. As a non-voting clerk of the Pennsylvania Assembly, he watched its construction, moving in the first day it was open, though not quite finished, in 1736. A half-century later, in 1787, Franklin was back in the State House, the oldest man with the youngest mind at the Constitutional Convention. The 2,000 pound bell cast in 1751 to keep time in the new tower was not really famous until the nineteenth century when African-Americans and, later, women used the Bell of Liberty as they pressed for the rights the original Constitution had omitted.*

▼▶ **Pennsylvania Academy of Fine Arts:** *Frank Furness' Victorian Gothic masterpiece on North Broad Street is home to America's first art museum and art school. His admixture of brownstone, brick, terracotta, stone columns, and sandstone carvings was completed in 1876. The curriculum was ahead of its time, featuring figure classes from both artists and leading physicians. Renowned artist Thomas Eakins, once a PAFA student himself, became director in 1882, but was dismissed for having nude male models in mixed classes. Distinguished alumni include Maxfield Parrish, Mary Cassatt, and Louis I. Kahn.*

the city's master builders, and to the First Continental Congress, which met there in 1774.

William Penn also insisted on "liberty of conscience" for his colony: complete religious freedom. With no established church to levy heavy tithes, Pennsylvania became the "best poor man's country." It attracted settlers, who hiked from other colonies seeking their fortunes in this land of opportunity, called "the strolling poor."

One of these was a runaway from Boston, who walked up Market Street on a Sunday in October of 1723, with three pennies in his pocket and an extra roll of damp socks. Twenty-five years later, Benjamin Franklin was able to take early retirement as an

eighteenth-century multimillionaire, to "join the free and easy society." He then made one of the world's great scientific discoveries, proving that electricity was a single "fluid" with what he termed both negative and positive forces.

Franklin was the most urban of the founding fathers. An avid reader and prolific writer, he enjoyed city life, declaring: "Conversation warms the Mind, enlivens the Imagination, and is continually starting fresh Game that is immediately pursu'd and taken." One of his first projects was to found the world's first lending library for working-class men. He realized that educated men would more readily stand up for their rights.

The "Great Communicator" of the eighteenth century, Franklin appreciated that words were his "principal means of advancement." His *Poor Richard's Almanack* and *Pennsylvania Gazette* were the most successful publications in the colonies. He even franchised his press, establishing others around the colonies. By the advent of the American Revolution, every major press was being operated by someone who could trace his training back to Franklin. Today, amid the Market Street block of rental properties once also owned by Franklin, the National Park Service gives demonstrations of eighteenth-century printing techniques.

Franklin also reorganized the postal service, riding throughout the colonies with an odometer attached to his wagon wheel to track distances so he could establish a fair system of guaranteed rates. Under his leadership, the Post Office even developed an overnight delivery system from Philadelphia to New York that was faster than the modern mail service. When relations between America and England deteriorated, the colonists relied on Franklin's communications network to support the War of Independence. Visitors can still mail a letter stamped in Benjamin Franklin's hand: "B. Free Franklin" at the U.S. Post Office in Franklin Court.

A generation older than the other founding fathers, Franklin set the tone for the group—establishing the infrastructure for a colonial union and

demonstrating the entrepreneurial spirit that would mark the new nation. However, when the curtain closed on the eighteenth century, Philadelphia's heady days as capital of the new nation also drew to an end, marked by two funerals. In 1790, Benjamin Franklin died in his courtyard home off Market Street. Over 20,000 people—the largest peacetime gathering in eighteenth-century America—attended his funeral. Nine years later Philadelphia hosted the new nation's official funeral of George Washington.

Perhaps no city in the world has a better claim on the eighteenth century. The most significant decisions on human rights, with global implications, took place in Philadelphia. Those glory years can be recaptured with a walk through the historic neighborhoods where America's founders spent their public lives, and where every street corner yields a Franklin discovery or invention.

In the nineteenth century, Philadelphia became the young nation's scientific and cultural hub. To prepare Merriweather Lewis for his exploration of the Louisiana territory, President Jefferson sent him to study with the top scientists at the American Philosophical Society on Fifth Street, founded by Franklin. The APS, the Nation's first "think tank," outfitted Lewis with three Conestoga wagons for the journey. When the Lewis and Clark Expedition ended, the specimens they collected were brought back to Philadelphia, and their journals housed at the Society.

The Athenaeum of Philadelphia, founded in 1814 by young professionals to celebrate the classics and "the useful arts," as Franklin termed them, built America's first Renaissance Revival building. It now holds the finest collection of architectural drawings and photographs in America, including Andrew Hamilton's original sketch of Independence Hall. As architect Benjamin Latrobe observed: "The days of Greece may be revived in the woods of America, and Philadelphia become the Athens of the Western World."

Chestnut Street Theatre, where Washington had enjoyed his favorite operas, was joined on the next block by the Walnut Street Theatre in 1809. On the second floor of Independence Hall, Charles Willson Peale established the country's first art museum, school of art, and natural history museum.

In the early eighteenth century, despite the Quakers, who considered music, dance, and theater "a waste of God's time," Philadelphia's musical scene had begun to flourish. Under the leadership of Benjamin Carr, who presided over the music at Washington's state funeral, Philadelphia became the musical capital of America. Founder of the first music publishing house, he also established the Musical Fund Society, America's first professional music society. In 1851, the Academy of Music was built in a quiet section of the city, at Broad and Locust streets. The plush interior of the "American La Scala" remains one of Philadelphia's great interior spaces.

Benjamin Franklin's publishing legacy flourished in the nineteenth century. Publishers like J.B. Lippincott, Charles J. Peterson with his *Saturday Evening Post*, and the Curtis publishing empire proclaimed the city's dominance. Edgar Allan Poe spent several years in an apartment near Spring Garden Street, composing the first mystery novels. Visitors can tour his house, now managed as a National Park site, and view the very raven that inspired his famous poem, stuffed and displayed in the rare book room of the Philadelphia Free Library. Another great American writer, Walt Whitman, spent his last decade in a small house across the Delaware River in Camden, revising *Leaves of Grass* and taking the ferry over to attend operas at the Academy of Music.

The institutions founded by Benjamin Franklin and his colleagues spawned many of America's premier scientific initiatives: the first operating room in the world at Pennsylvania Hospital; the world's first school of pharmacy; America's initial journals in botany and medicine; the world's first medical school for women; and Jefferson Medical College, whose highly-regarded staff has graduated more physicians than any other institution in the world. John Bartram's eighteenth-century garden, still located on the west bank of the Schuylkill, and his studies of

▶ **City Hall at Night:** *This dazzling display of light dramatizes the Classical and Beaux Arts elements that make Philadelphia City Hall a gargantuan work of art. The lights are one of the many initiatives by the Center City District to turn Center City into a welcoming and stimulating environment.*

flora and fauna, aided the development of the pharmaceutical industry and helped lay the groundwork for ornithology. John James Audubon began his work on his aunt's estate near Philadelphia. The Franklin Institute was founded in 1824 to promote scientific progress, and throughout the nineteenth century, scientists at the Institute conducted educational programs and competitions for inventors.

Arts, sciences, and letters aside, Philadelphia also became the axis of America's Industrial Revolution. Encouraged by the most populist of founding fathers, the city was transformed into America's great blue-collar center of manufacturing. In 1822, Frederick Graff engineered the world's first citywide gravity-fed water distribution system at Fairmount on the Schuylkill River. Philadelphia also developed

▼ **Fairmount Waterworks:** *"The Waterworks, which are on a height near the city, are no less ornamental than useful,"* the English novelist Charles Dickens wrote in 1840, with *"fresh water jerked about, turned on, and poured off everywhere."* Now that the reservoir has been supplanted by the Philadelphia Museum of Art on the brow of the hill, these restored Palladian structures contribute their man-made beauty to the natural wonders of Fairmount Park.

into a railroad city. Matthias Baldwin, the first American manufacturer, expanded his locomotive works into the largest in the world. Now familiar as a stop on the Monopoly board, the Reading Railroad was one of the first rail lines in the country. Another of the city's industrialists, Joseph Harrison, Jr. expanded into the international market, constructing railroad engines, cars, and track for Czarist Russia. As rails stretched across the United States, the major lines all crossed at the roundhouse in Philadelphia. In 1882, the world's largest train depot was built next to City Hall.

Philadelphia had become the world's largest manufacturer for hundreds of products, from streetcars, trolleys, and cable cars to Disston saws. Over 600 mills turned out textiles, while others made cigars, candy, leather, pharmaceuticals, paint, sugar, and machine tools. Even the symbol of the Wild West, the "ten gallon" Stetson cowboy hat, was made in Philadelphia. During the Civil War, the city was the single largest supplier of Union Army uniforms and munitions. Many corporations also helped supply the Southern army.

In troubled times, Americans have often turned to Philadelphia and the great symbols of the Nation's beginnings. For example, the city was enlisted to help heal the wounds caused by the Civil War. The Liberty Bell, a national symbol acceptable to both North and South, was placed on an open railroad car and taken around to all the states.

Philadelphia provided even deeper healing during America's Centennial, when it hosted the first successful world's fair on American soil. A full quarter of the nation's population came to Fairmount Park in 1876, visiting 200 buildings, including the world's largest structure, the twenty-three-acre Main Exhibition Hall. It was the first chance for the public to see a typewriter, Mr. Bell's telephone, and sample Hires Root Beer. The enormous fairground was even connected to the city by its own railroad. Memorial Hall, one of the only permanent buildings in the fair, still stands in the park.

Philadelphia marked the end of the nineteenth century with a new City Hall, the world's largest masonry building, with walls twenty-two-feet thick and 650-feet long. Begun in 1872, it was intended to be not only the largest, but also the tallest building

on the planet. It still dominates Center City as America's finest example of French Second Empire architecture, and is one big reason that Philadelphia is rated among the world's five best cities for Victorian-era architecture. On January 1, 1900, at the stroke of midnight, 12,000 light bulbs, strung from the statue of William Penn, were switched on to help Philadelphia usher in the twentieth century.

One block east of City Hall, John Wanamaker was building the largest department store anywhere, with two million square feet of floor space. The pipes of the world's largest organ still line one wall of its seven-story atrium. After the colonial market arcade was demolished, shoppers could take the trolley down Market Street to their favorite stores: the Lit Brothers, Strawbridge and Clothier, Macy's, and Gimbels, sponsor of America's first Thanksgiving Day Parade.

Despite popular conception, it was not Hollywood, but Philadelphia that blazed a trail for the American movie industry. In 1915, the Lubin studio distributed 2,000 silent films worldwide. When barbed wire threw cowhands out of work, they were hired by the studio to rustle cattle and rob stagecoaches along the Schuylkill River. The recording industry also enjoyed its infancy here: the Great Caruso and other famous opera singers appearing at the Academy of Music were ferried across the Delaware to record for Johnson's Victor Talking Machine in Camden. Under the leadership of Leopold Stokowski, the Philadelphians became the first recorded orchestra in the world.

When Horn and Hardart opened their first automat in Philadelphia, it signalled the official birth to the fast food industry. Waterfront workers were now toting their meat and cheese hoagies to work on Hog Island. When World War I broke out, Philadelphia's shipbuilders increased their production to support the war effort, as they did again in World War II. In one month alone nearly 400 ships were ordered at the Philadelphia and Camden docks, from troop carriers to the mightiest of battleships like the U.S.S. *New Jersey.* The Philadelphia region provided more ships for the two wars than any other in America.

Between the wars, the city took steps to connect Fairmount Park to Center City with the Benjamin

Kimmel Center: *Internationally renowned architect Rafael Vinoly built this expanded version of the classic Roman arch from glass to enclose two concert spaces; the cello-shaped, exotic wood-paneled Verizon Hall, home of the world renowned Philadelphia Orchestra, and the intimate Perelman Theatre. Vinoly explained: "You have to make a landmark for a city of monuments." This exciting building is the centerpiece of the five-block section of Broad Street immediately south of City Hall, now dubbed "Avenue of the Arts."*

Franklin Parkway. *The Ladies' Home Journal* and the *Saturday Evening Post*, with its Norman Rockwell covers, dominated the news stands. America applauded such Philadelphia stars as John, Ethel, and Lionel Barrymore, as well as film greats W.C. Fields, Jeannette Macdonald, and Nelson Eddy. Marion Anderson's public concert on the Washington Mall was broadcast nationwide.

In keeping with the city's traditions of pioneering thought, the world's first computer (ENIAC) was switched on here in 1944. It filled a room at the University of Pennsylvania's school of engineering. Three years later another very Philadelphian group was awarded the Nobel Peace Prize for work on behalf of European refugees in both world wars.

The American Friends Service Committee, headquartered in Philadelphia, were the action arm of the Quakers.

In other ways the twentieth century proved a more difficult time for Philadelphia. The Depression after the first war and the decline of American industry after the second left sections of the city devastated, but reform mayors Clark and Dilworth, with visionary city planner Edmund Bacon, successfully enlivened other sections of William Penn's grid. Society Hill was restored to its colonial splendor. The forbidding stone wall that had shuttled steam locomotives through the heart of the city was demolished in favor of Thirtieth Street Station by the Schuylkill River. Modern office buildings began to sprout along the newly opened corridor.

Philadelphia also continued to contribute more than its share of talent to the entertainment industries. Cool beauty Grace Kelly and brilliant tenor Mario Lanza became international stars and South Philadelphian crooners; Al Martino, Chubby Checker, and Fabian were also hugely successful. The city even became a movie star in its own right, as the film industry capitalized on Philadelphia's striking architecture and natural settings to produce some of its biggest hits: *Rocky* with Sylvester Stallone, *Trading Places* starring Eddie Murphy, *Blow Out* with John Travolta, *Witness* starring Harrison Ford, *Philadelphia* starring Tom Hanks, and *The Sixth Sense* written by Philadelphia's own M. Night Shyamalan.

The city with the most populist of founding fathers also has its own public art. Creative city leaders converted the graffiti problem into an artistic solution, and now over 2,400 buildings boast colorful murals, many of them painted with assistance from neighborhood youths. Artist Isaiah Zagar has also brightened South Street with shimmering tile-and-mirror mosaics, but even before the murals, Philadelphia contained more public art than any other city in the world.

Philadelphia is still a national center for medicine and health, and two of its first-rate medical institutions can be traced back to Benjamin Franklin— Pennsylvania Hospital and the University of Pennsylvania, with its renowned children's hospital. Many of the nation's leading pharmaceutical and insurance firms are also based in the city where the Hand In Hand Insurance Co., founded by Franklin, still thrives as America's oldest corporation. The city scene is also brightened by one of the largest college populations in America—more than 300,000 college students attend the region's eighty-four colleges.

Under Mayor Edward G. Rendell's exuberant leadership in the 1990s, the city took stock of its unmatched heritage and architectural treasures, and launched a campaign to become a top tourist destination. Taking up the challenge, Greater Philadelphia Tourism Marketing Corporation has collaborated in helping millions of new visitors feel welcome.

Benjamin Franklin would be delighted to see the new life in his home city still generating fresh ideas over two centuries after his death. And William Penn would also be proud of the success of his city of brotherly love, and of the incredible contributions its citizens have made to progress and peace.

Old City / New City

Old City Philadelphia boasts the oldest residential street in America, Elfreth's Alley, just around the corner from the Clay Studio, one of fifty hip art galleries that fling open their doors on First Friday evenings for the best monthly block party in the East. Art collectors with serious cash mingle with fashionable students at openings, dine alfresco near street musicians, or seek a civilized corner in Washington's pew at Christ Church, on Second near Market Street, for a free concert. Described as the "liveliest urban neighborhood" between Manhattan and Miami, Old City provides an assurance of Philadelphia's continuing vibrancy.

The western edge of Old City is anchored by two modern buildings, the Visitor Center at Sixth and Market Streets and the National Constitution Center at Sixth and Arch Streets. Sitting over a three-level underground parking garage, the Visitor Center is a convenient and friendly way for guests of the city to get their bearings. Staff from Philadelphia's tourist office and rangers for Independence Historic National Park stand ready to provide information on virtually any Philadelphia subject or site.

Described as the "best new American museum," the only one designed to celebrate the nation's most important document, the National Constitution Center offers interactive exhibits for adults, as well as school groups. Its exciting multimedia show helps to bring the constitution to life, and its roomful of life-sized constitutional signers is an engaging experience.

Old City's exciting restaurant scene includes Buddakan and Cuba Libre, as well as one of the city's famed Victorian interiors, the beautifully restored Bourse. This historically rich neighborhood has appeared on MTV, in the movies *Beloved* and *The Sixth Sense*, and in an earlier century spawned the Philadelphia Orchestra. Whether enjoying the Arden Theatre at night or historic sites like the Betsy Ross House by day, visitors as well as residents will find something to interest them at every turn.

▶ **The Bourse:** *Built in 1895 as America's first commodities exchange, the Bourse stretches a city block from Fourth Street to Fifth, across the street from the Liberty Bell Pavilion. The building was restored to its Victorian splendor of polished brass balconies and ornate plasterwork in 1982. Philadelphia is a city of great spaces, and the interior of the Bourse ranks with the best. Its mix of shops and eateries serves thousands of visitors each day.*

▲ Betsy Ross House:

*Whether or not Betsy Ross
sewed the first American flag
in this house, visitors can still
see how she lived on the
second block of Mulberry
Street—now named Arch
Street because of the bridge
near the river front. They will
also learn how this twenty-
something spitfire joined the
Revolutionary cause, and
rediscover a woman who
survived three husbands to
manage her own successful
business.*

▶ Elfreth's Alley:

*America's oldest residential
street, at over 300 years old,
may seem quaint to the
millions who visit it, but it was
simply a home and work
space in the eighteenth
century. Mary Smith ran her
dressmaking shop from
number 126, and Moses
Mordicai, founding member of
the city's first synagogue, lived
in 118. Cuff Douglas, a free
black tailor, worked at 117,
while the Quaker shipwright
Israel Cassel in 124 supplied
boats to evacuate wounded
soldiers from the Brandywine
battlefield in 1777.*

▶ **Christ Church:** *Fresh from erecting the elegant Wren churches after London's Great Fire, the master builders of Philadelphia's Carpenters Company proudly created the finest Georgian building in America. Benjamin Franklin ran three lotteries to fund its steeple, less from devotion than the need for a promontory to test his theories on lightning.*

◀ **Poe House:** *The rear portion of the house on Seventh Street where Poe rented rooms was the site for his first mysteries. Today, National Park rangers delight in taking visitors to the basement to see the bricked-in area that inspired one of his chilliest tales. Poe may have composed The Raven in the house, though the real bird actually belonged to another writer, Charles Dickens, who joined Edgar Allan Poe for dinner on his visit to Philadelphia. In fact, Grip the Raven is stuffed and displayed in the Philadelphia Free Library.*

▶ **Christ Church, interior:** *The magnificent Palladian window of Christ Church is considered the first and best in the colonies. On Sunday mornings in the 1790s, President and Mrs. Washington would alight at Second and Market from their grand coach to join the congregation.*

◀ **National Constitution Center:** *America's best new interactive museum celebrates America's most successful export: more than 200 other governments have adopted features from the United States Constitution. The center's multimedia show is a must-see, and even the most foot-weary of historic hikers are moved when they mingle among the life-sized statues of the Constitution's signers.*

▲ **Old City's First Friday:** *Old City's colonial icons such as Elfreth's Alley and Betsy Ross House are surrounded by five-story warehouses, monuments to a bustling nineteenth-century commercial era. In the 1960s and 70s, these warehouses offered inexpensive lofts for artists, with the result that today's Old City is an exciting mix of over fifty art galleries and Bohemian restaurants. On the first Friday of each month, the galleries open their doors for an evening of art, music, and street theater.*

◄ **Arden Theatre:**
Since its founding in 1988,
the theater has mounted
over ninety productions,
including twenty-four world
premieres. It has a reputation
for creating successful stage
works from poetry, nonfiction,
and fiction, such as Kurt
Vonnegut's short stories.
Located on Second Street
next to Christ Church, it is an
integral part of Old City's
vibrant nightlife.

▲ **Cuba Libre:** This
stylish recreation of Old
Havana's city square is one
of Philadelphia's most
popular celebration
restaurants. Diners are
surrounded by interesting
architecture, played mood-
inducing music, and treated
with exceptional food. Cuba
Libre's Rum Bar is the perfect
finish. It is located at 10
South Second Street, on the
edge of Old City.

Society Hill

Cobblestone lanes, graced by Benjamin Franklin's street lamps, crisscross the world's largest intact neighborhood of English colonial townhouses in America's most historic square mile. Their sheer elegance merit a stroll into the eighteenth-century world that Vice President John Adams, an inveterate walker, trod on many an evening. Although now he might not recognize the Pine Street Presbyterian Church, "modernized" in the 1840s with an elaborate columned front portico. When it resounded with Reverand Duffield's fire and brimstone sermons, like the ones he was used to in New England, Adams rarely missed a Sunday. He would, of course, be right at home in the City Tavern on Second Street, where he dined the minute he arrived for the 1774 congressional meetings. Even before he was able to drop his luggage across the street in Mrs. Yard's rooming house, he was treated to "the finest meal ever laid upon a table."

Carpenters Hall, still owned by the Worshipful Carpenters Company of Philadelphia, which was the impromptu meeting place for the First Continental Congress, presides over the third block of Chestnut Street, across from Benjamin Franklin's courtyard. Wealthy, retired from printing, and poised to return to England to press for America's rights, Franklin decided to build his "good house" in the heart of the city. Evidence of his immeasurable influence over his city and his century are everywhere. The reconstructed Library Company building, with the statue of Franklin in a toga perched over the front door, is the repository for many of his personal letters and belongings, including one of the scientist's famous batteries.

▶ **Merchants Exchange:** *Designed by Philadelphian William Strickland, the Merchants Exchange is located at Third and Walnut Streets. The semicircular Greek Revival portico graces one of America's first Classical Revival buildings, the architecture that the United States adopted to trace its founding principles back to Athens and the Roman Senate. Its tower permitted an early version of insider trading—young men were sent up the winding stairs to sight the ships sailing into harbor. The oldest stock market building in America, it now houses the northeastern headquarters of the National Park Service.*

◀ **Fourth and Prune:**
Now a beautifully landscaped corner lot, this is where the future King of France, Louis-Phillippe, shared a house with his brother before being returned to the crown. The house on the south corner was home to Dr. William Shippen, head of medical services for the Revolutionary army. After his death, it was occupied by Dr. Caspar Wistar, head of the American Philosophical Society and scientific mentor to Merriweather Lewis.

▲ **Old Swedes (Gloria Dei Church):** Built in 1699 on the bank of the Delaware River, this is the oldest church building in Pennsylvania. Its most prominent Swedish pastor was Nils Collin, a good friend of Benjamin Franklin. The attempt to tame lightning with Franklin's lightning rods was considered by many as an affront to God, but Collin still installed them on his church. Vestiges of those first rods can still be seen on this National Historic Site, located on Columbus Boulevard at Christian Street.

▲ **Old Pine Street Church:** *"Old Pine," near Third Street, is the oldest Presbyterian church in continuous use in America. The church was controlled by the "old order" First Presbyterian Church, until the popular young minister had his first child only six months after his wedding. He was removed for "antenuptial fornication."*

The congregation instead defiantly chose their own "New Light" minister, George Duffield, whose fiery sermons appealed to John Adams as more nearly resembling "those of our New England Clergy." In the nineteenth century the wealthy congregation added elaborate Corinthian columns as part of its new Classical Revival facade.

▶ **Powel House:** *The plain Quaker-built exterior of America's finest Georgian townhouse belies its elaborate interior. After Samuel Powel purchased it for his bride in 1769, he hired Robert Smith to redecorate the inside with arches, pediments, and molding. Powel and the witty, loquacious Eliza hosted lavish dinner parties and dances for*

Franklin, Washington, Lafayette, and Jefferson. John Adams even complained in his diary: "Another sinfull feast at the Powel House— 20 types of tarts, beer, wine, syllabub." The exquisitely restored house on Third Street is one of four historic houses maintained and open to the public under the auspices of the Philadelphia Landmarks Society.

◀ **Carpenters Hall:**
Designed by America's first great builder, Philadelphian Robert Smith, this guild hall still belongs to the Worshipful Carpenters Company of Philadelphia. It was finished just in time to host the First Continental Congress in 1774. Franklin's library on the second floor was used by the delegates as the first "congressional library." Here Colonel George Washington and John Adams collaborated on the colonists' rights, while Patrick Henry unfurled his impressive oratory: "I am not a Virginian, but an American."

▲ **Newmarket:** *The 1745 New Market on Second Street was built for the residents of Society Hill. Market days were big events, especially if a hanging was scheduled. Window shoppers were a problem even in colonial times, especially once women began to wear hoop skirts. Gossiping instead of purchasing, they clogged up the aisles and kept shoppers from the farmers' rented stalls. The frustrated Pennsylvania farmers solved the gridlock by occasionally letting frogs loose in the aisle, scattering the gossipers.*

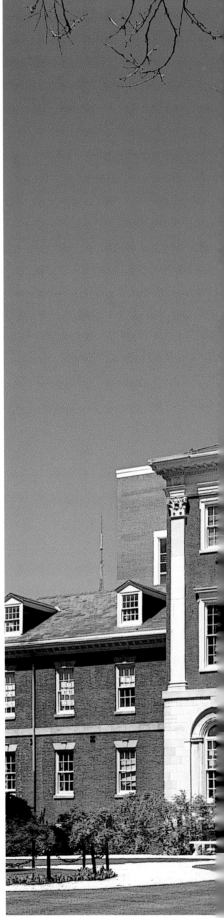

▲ **Franklin Court:** *In 1761, Benjamin Franklin began constructing his "good house," set back from Market Street. He enjoyed city life too much to have a sedate country home, but he wanted to avoid the noises and smells of the city. He situated his "country" house in a courtyard surrounded by trees and flowers, while a row of townhouses on the street served as a buffer. The space once occupied by Franklin's house is now marked by Robert Venturi's architectural sculpture, completed in 1976.*

▶ **Pennsylvania Hospital:** *Benjamin Franklin used the concept of "matching funds" to talk the Pennsylvania Assembly into promising half of the money for America's first hospital "for the relief of the sick poor and for the reception and cure of lunaticks." Never expecting Franklin to raise his half of the costs, the Assembly hoped for "the credit of being charitable without the expense." Franklin succeeded however, and the building was erected at the corner of Eighth and Pine Streets in 1756.*

▶ **Abercrombie House:** *In 1759 Captain Abercrombie built the grandest four-story town house in Philadelphia, on Second Street just north of Spruce Street. Beautifully restored, this building now shares Society Hill with three condominium towers designed by renowned architect I. M. Pei in 1964.*

◀ **City Tavern:** *In 1774, when John Adams arrived in Philadelphia for a congressional meeting, before he could drop his luggage at Mrs. Yard's rooming house, he was ushered across Second Street to City Tavern for "the finest meal ever laid upon a table." Built in 1773 to reflect the city's status as the largest and richest in the colonies, the City Tavern was America's first gourmet restaurant. The present City Tavern is a faithful reconstruction maintained by Independence National Park, offering authentic colonial cuisine, brought to the table by waiters in colonial garb.*

▶ **Second Bank:** *William Strickland designed the Second Bank building in 1824. It became a prototype for banks around the country, but now hosts an exhibit celebrating early nineteenth-century Philadelphia as the Athens of America. The red brick building adjacent to the bank is the library housing rare colonial documents for the American Philosophical Society.*

▶ **First Bank:** *America's First Bank building is located on Third Street. Washington's Secretary of the Treasury, Alexander Hamilton, resided nearby, on the corner of Third and Chestnut. A leading proponent of big government, he had more staff on this single block than the other three cabinet members combined.*

◀ **Philadelphia City Hall:** *When the poet Walt Whitman saw Philadelphia City Hall, still under construction, by the light of a full moon, he called it, "silent, weird, beautiful." Others insisted it was an appalling marble elephant. If the price of demolishing it had not matched that of erecting it, the world's largest and most expensive nineteenth-century building might not now dominate the center of William Penn's city grid. The artwork in the foreground is Claes Oldenburg's 1976 sculpture* Clothespin.

▶ **Wanamaker/Lord and Taylor:** *The Wanamaker Department Store began to rise in 1902 next to Philadelphia's new City Hall. Like a Renaissance palace, its exterior is unadorned, while the interior is eye-popping. On its completion, John Wanamaker had the largest department store in the world, with two million square feet of floor space and a seven-story atrium holding the world's largest pipe organ. He also installed an enormous bronze eagle on the atrium floor, noting that, unlike other merchants, he was not a wren but an eagle. This is one of Philadelphians' favorite meeting spots, and the store's Christmas show is a favorite holiday treat.*

▲ **Lit Brothers:** *The graceful Renaissance Revival Lit Brothers building, which covers Market Street from Seventh to Eighth Streets, consists of eleven sections gradually acquired or built as the Lit family's clothing store expanded. Saved from demolition in 1977, this grand structure now contains offices on the upper floors and discount shopping at street level.*

◀ **Loews Hotel/Market East:** *This view of Market Street East includes the Art Deco facade of the Loews Hotel. Erected in 1932, this was America's first International Style skyscraper, a "summation of European Modernism." It was the headquarters for the first savings bank in the nation, the Philadelphia Saving Fund Society.*

▲ **Taller Puertorriqueno:** *Home to Philadelphia's collection of Puerto Rican and other Latin American visual arts, the Taller Puertorriqueno is the city's foremost Latino educational and performance space. Located at 2721 North Fifth Street, it anchors a residential neighborhood of people from every Latin country, offering unique shops, friendly restaurants, concerts, and special festivals. One of Philadelphia's famous murals covers the north wall.*

▲ **Chinatown:** Just steps from the Pennsylvania Convention Center, this compact neighborhood of Chinese residents, cultural sites, and shops boasts many of America's finest, most "authentic" Chinese restaurants. Other Asian cultures have also made their mark on these blocks. A beloved Philadelphia landmark, the spectacular Chinatown Friendship Gate on Tenth Street near Arch is the first authentic Chinese gate built in America by artisans from China.

▶ **Reading Terminal:** In 1893, the Reading Railroad built its head house at Twelfth and Market Streets. The massive railroad shed, which is the largest single-span structure in the world, is connected to the rear of the building. The tracks were removed to create a grand entrance to Philadelphia's Convention Center. At street level, underneath the grand shed, America's oldest continuously operating indoor market boasts 100 stalls serving up everything from freshly-made pretzels and Amish-grown produce to gourmet lunches.

▶ **Mural Arts:**
Established in 1984 as part
of an anti-graffiti initiative,
Philadelphia's Mural Arts
Program originally redirected
the creative energies of select
graffiti writers into projects to
enhance their communities.
Since that off-beat beginning,
the project has grown to
include many of the region's
finest artists, in cooperation
with neighborhoods that host
over 2,400 murals. Popular
trolley tours offer a look at
selected murals.

◀ **Temple University:**
The modern bell tower on
the library plaza proclaims a
modern center city university
that balances quality with
accessibility for both urban
and suburban students in the
Philadelphia region. It offers a
rich array of academic
programs, from the arts and
sciences to law school,
medical school, and allied
medical careers.

▶ **Rittenhouse**
Square: *In 1825, this most*
neglected of William Penn's
original five city squares was
named in honor of America's
first astronomer, David
Rittenhouse. During the
1850s it saw a building
boom, as wealthy indust-
rialists left the crowded
eighteenth-century side of the
city and sought out places for
their mansions. In 1913, the
residents funded this design
for the square by the noted
French architect Paul Cret.

University of Pennsylvania, Benjamin Franklin Statue: *America's first non-denominational college began its life as the Academy of Philadelphia, founded in 1749 by Benjamin Franklin. Insisting on "everything that is useful," along with the classics, his college was the first to use English as the primary language. Today, students can still sit next to the great man and while away a few minutes between classes.*

University of Pennsylvania: *This great Ivy League university offers many top-rated academic programs, including the Wharton School of Finance and Commerce, the first and most prestigious business school in the country. Its Museum of Archaeology is justly renowned, as is its Children's Hospital. The lively urban campus attracts students from around the globe.*

World Café: *This modern building nestled in the ivied campus of the University of Pennsylvania is the very modern World Café Live. A unique collaboration between WXPN, the University's nationally broadcast public radio station, and a concert presenter, the facility boasts two restaurants and a lively concert venue.*

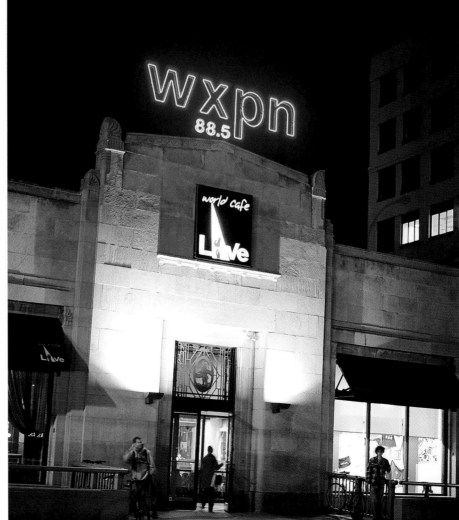

▲ **Franklin Statue:**
*Philadelphia has thirty major
pieces of public art honoring
its most famous son, including
this whimsical abstract of the
face that was, by his own
account, "more famous than
the side of the moon." This
artwork presides over the
Vine Street Expressway at
street level near the grand
parkway named in his honor.
In the photo, it frames the
tower of the city's leading
newspaper,* The Philadelphia
Inquirer, *a fitting tribute for
the man who published the
most successful newspaper in
colonial America, invented the
editorial page, and drew
America's first political
cartoon.*

▶ **Thirtieth Street
Station:** *Completed during
the Great Depression, this
is one of the nation's last
grand railroad stations, and
a testament to the city's
prominence in the national
railway system. Even today,
regardless of direction, East
Coast travelers must come
through Philadelphia. This
photograph also shows
creatively lit bridges across
the Schuylkill River, with the
gleaming new Circa Center
office building, designed by
Cesar Pelli, behind the station.*

Fairmount Park

The pleasures of the Fairmount Park area beckoned Philadelphians well before the current crop of joggers, cyclists, bladers, and picnickers. Indeed, one June, in order to honor Colonel Washington a few days before he took command of the Patriot Army, Benjamin Franklin attempted to roast a turkey on an electrical spit for a picnic on the Schuylkill.

The eighteenth century was a time of fishing clubs and men's clubs along the river. Wealthy colonists like Mayor Samuel Powel and the privateer Macpherson also built grand country houses along its pristine bank, escaping from the turgid air and foul streets of the closely-packed city in the summer.

Fairmount Park took full shape in the nineteenth century. Beginning at the base of the small hill, Faire Mount, five acres were acquired and landscaped around that mechanical wonder of the century, the Philadelphia Waterworks. Additional land was purchased in 1828 and 1844 to protect the purity of the water being pumped up to the reservoir on the top of the hill. Clean water from American's first complete gravity-feed city water system flowed throughout the city, terminating in dog's best friend, the fire hydrant.

Developed in time to host a world's fair in honor of the nation's centennial, Fairmount Park had grown to 9,000 acres, the largest single urban park in the world. It still contains several of the original 200-plus centennial buildings, including the magnificent Memorial Hall, now an interactive museum for children. The park is also home to America's first zoo, now topped off with a "zoo balloon." The Fairmount Park Art Association has contributed significantly to Philadelphia's status as the top city in the world for public art. It has adorned the park with hundreds of artworks, from monuments of presidents to the Catholic Abstinence Fountain sculpted for the Centennial Exposition. Lincoln signing the Emancipation Proclamation and General Grant on his horse are on the eastern side of the Schuylkill near Laurel Hill Cemetery, which is filled with the tombs of Civil War personalities like General Meade.

Today, Fairmount Park, beginning just steps from the Museum of Art, is Philadelphia's "Great Outdoors." People of all ages and shapes, from grannies on bikes to hip-hop picnickers, college rowers to kissing couples, can be found on the park's trails and grassy knolls.

▶ **Mount Pleasant, aerial view:** *Seven eighteenth-century country houses are open to the public in Fairmount Park, but Mount Pleasant is generally regarded as the finest of them and, indeed, the best example of a Georgian country house in America. It was built on a prospect overlooking the Schuylkill river, and has two front doors— one for the river and one facing the long rutted drive from colonial Philadelphia.*

◀ **Mount Pleasant:**
Built in 1761 for Captain
John Macpherson, a Scottish
Privateer, it was purchased
during the Revolutionary War
by Benedict Arnold for his
bride, Peggy Shippen.

▲ **Remington
Sculpture:** Frederic
Remington was
commissioned to produce a
bronze sculpture of a horse
and cowboy for Fairmount
Park in 1905, a time when
the Lubin Corporation was
filming Western movies along
the western bank of the
Schuylkill River. He chose a
rocky ledge on the eastern
side of the river for the only
large-scale sculpture he
would ever produce. The
result is considered one of
the world's great kinetic
studies. The horse, its foreleg
flung outward, has pulled up
short after a furious gallop, at
the edge of a precipice. Its
rugged rider, with a full
handlebar moustache, is
completely one with his
horse, a study of trust and
confidence in the saddle.

▲ **Valley Green Inn:**
The inn, built in 1850, is
located on Forbidden Drive
along the Wissahickon Creek.
It was once a favorite stop
for winter sleighing parties
and summer carriage rides,
but today it is cyclists, joggers,
and hikers who stop for a
relaxing bite on the front
porch. Riders are also catered
for—there is a handy shed
nearby where their steeds
can rest. Restored on several
occasions, most recently in
2002, the Inn's quaint
surroundings are ideal for a
romantic dinner.

▶ **Columbia Bridge:**
The first bridge at this
location was built in 1834 to
carry tracks across to the
base of the Belmont Plateau,
where a stationary engine
pulled freight cars up the
steep grade on route to the
Pennsylvania coal mines.
When the current Columbia
Bridge was completed in
1921, its rails carried
passenger cars to the
Reading Head House and
shed on Market Street in
Center City.

◀ **Grant Sculpture:**

Another equestrian masterpiece on the east side of the Schuylkill, this monument to General Ulysses S. Grant by sculptor Daniel Chester French captures the awesome moment of Union victory over the Confederate troops. It depicts a solemn, firm, quietly alert Grant, motionless on his horse, surveying the battlefield. The horse too stands quietly, its head down. Together, their posture expresses a mood of uneasy calm and latent strength. Many sculptures in Fairmount Park honor Civil War figures, including President Lincoln, poised to sign his Emancipation Proclamation.

▲ **Memorial Hall/
Centennial Hall:**

Philadelphia hosted America's first successful world's fair, erecting over 200 structures in Fairmount Park to celebrate the centennial of the nation. These included the world's largest structure, the twenty-three-acre Main Exhibition Building; twenty-four individual Victorian buildings for each State; fifteen international buildings, including the first exhibition of Japanese culture in America; and Memorial Hall, the central building. At the time it was so highly admired that it became the model for Germany's Reichstag. Memorial Hall now houses a popular interactive children's museum.

▲ **Japanese House and Garden:** *A Japanese structure has stood on this ground since the first ever exhibit of Japanese culture in America at the 1876 Centennial Exposition. The*

Japanese House and Garden, designed in sixteenth-century style, was built in 1953 in Nagoya and reassembled in Philadelphia in 1958. It is considered skoin-zukuri, a desk-centered house.

◄▲ Philadelphia Zoo:

*Fairmount joggers and cyclists
share their park with
Canadian geese, wild deer,
urban cowboys on tall horses,
millions of squirrels, and
1,600 rare and exotic
animals. The latter spend
their days on the forty-two
acres of America's first zoo.
The Philadelphia Zoo
features a special primate
reserve, a rare animal
conservation center, a reptile
and amphibian house, and a
special children's section with
a giant tree house. Visitors
who prefer to be above it all
can take a ride in the Zoo
Balloon.*

◀ **Bartram's Garden:**

The stone house John Bartram built nearly three centuries ago still overlooks the experimental garden this pioneer botanist grew on the banks of the Schuylkill River. Bartram and his son William traveled the length of the English colonies, from Lake Ontario to Florida, collecting seedlings, shrubs, and plants. He also studied Latin with James Logan, so that he could identify and name his plants. Thomas Jefferson once spent several weeks here studying Bartram's techniques. Visitors today will see an example of the rare flowering tree Franklinia Altamaha, named in honor of John Bartram's friend.

▲ **Playing Angels:**

Perched on top of 20-foot columns, these three bronze-sculpted angels were created by Carl Milles. The original five overlook Stockholm's harbor, but three of the second cast were purchased for Fairmount Park. These cheerful creatures dance while they make music, reminding visitors to the park that life is a celebration.

◀ **Strawberry Mansion Bridge:**

Constructed in 1897, the Strawberry Mansion Bridge spans the Schuylkill with a beautiful series of steel arches. The 1,227-foot-long bridge was originally intended to carry trolleys as part of a nine-mile trolley system, but recently received a facelift to accommodate pedestrian and light vehicular traffic.

▲ **East Falls Bridge:**

The Lenape Indians called this small rapids in the Schuylkill Ganshewhanna, meaning noisy waters. As early as 1732, the Fort St. David's Fishing Club jutted over the rapids, anchored to flat rocks. It included a museum of "foreign and domestic curiosities," which were plundered by the Hessian troops when the British took

Philadelphia in 1777. The first bridge was made of chain in 1808, but after it washed away, the nation's first wire suspension bridge was erected in its place. In only six months, this bridge too was washed away by snow and ice. The East Falls Bridge, built in 1895, is the sixth, a powerful variation of a Pratt truss, designed to handle a second level if needed.

▲ ▶ **Laurel Hill Cemetery:** *One of the first landscaped cemeteries in the country, Laurel Hill is rich with impressive mausoleums and funereal art. After it was developed in 1836, it attracted over 30,000 picnickers a year, becoming so popular that the cemetery implemented a ticket system to keep from becoming overrun. Many of nineteenth-century Philadelphia's industrial magnates, like Disston and Weidener, as well as Civil War figures such as George Meade, are buried on Laurel Hill.*

▲ **Belmont Plateau:**
Named for Belmont Mansion,
a farmhouse built by the
Peters family, the plateau
offers one of the most
beautiful vistas of the
cityscape in the distance. So
many people came to enjoy
the view that in 1870 a
restaurant was established at
the mansion.

▶ **Boathouse Row at
Night:** After the Schuylkill
River was dammed, the
becalmed river became a
world-famous sculling
waterway. An elegant row of
Victorian Gothic boathouses
soon grew along the river
bend, including the Undine
Barge Club designed by
Frank Furness. The Schuylkill
Navy, the oldest sports

organization in the English-
speaking world, was founded
here in 1858. Each May the
Dad Vail Regatta still draws
the top college rowing teams
to America's largest
championship meet. The
special lights, which started
as an act of whimsy during a
holiday season, have become
one of Philadelphia's most
popular postcard images.

The Parkway and Avenue of Arts

Visitors can walk along the Benjamin Franklin Parkway past a bonanza of visual arts institutions to City Hall, and pivot down South Broad Street, where Philadelphia's most prominent performance spaces are situated. This two-mile stretch is one of the greatest concentrations of the fine arts in the world. With the addition of the Barnes Foundation, it has few rivals.

The Parkway was carved diagonally through the northwest quadrant of Penn's colonial grid, connecting the Philadelphia Museum of Art to City Hall in the early twentieth century. Many of the city's major museums are arrayed along this mile and a half of tree-lined avenue, Philadelphia's Champs Elysée. Visitors can enjoy the premier collection of American art in the nation's first art museum, the Pennsylvania Academy of Fine Arts, then continue past the great Classical Revival library and court-house at the Logan Circle Fountain and on to the amazing sculptures at the Rodin Museum. The other side of the Parkway boasts the Museum of Natural History, with its collection of flora and fauna from the Lewis and Clark expedition, and the renowned Franklin Institute.

Under the leadership of Mayor Edward Rendell, Broad Street just south of City Hall has been restored to a modern version of its early nineteenth-century style and renamed the Avenue of the Arts. The Academy of Music shares its musical duties with the brilliant glass-arched performing arts center, the Kimmel Center, now home to the Philadelphia Orchestra. New buildings for jazz and theatrical productions are clustered on the avenue close to the University of the Arts.

▶ **Philadelphia Museum of Art:** *One of the world's largest Classical Revival buildings, the museum sits atop Faire Mount. Although one member of the museum's board called it "that great Greek garage," it is regarded as one of the city's great architectural gems. Ever since the Rocky movies, the museum's "Rocky steps" have been a tourist magnet. The museum also hosts the city's most spectacular concert and fireworks shows every July 4.*

◀ **Barnes Foundation:** *Among Philadelphia's brilliant and generous eccentrics, Dr. Albert C. Barnes holds a premier position. After amassing a sizable fortune from a pharmaceutical discovery, he embarked on an extraordinary artistic odyssey. The result is a quirky museum bursting with one of the largest collections of impressionist art in the world, interspersed with local Pennsylvania folk furniture and African art.*

▶ **Victor Café:** *This old Philadelphia icon was originally Victor DiStefano's gramophone shop in 1918. In the 1930s, however, DiStefano opened an Italian restaurant, which became a must for opera legends who visited the city, from Caruso to Pavarotti. Even after Mario Lanza became famous, he would return to his old neighborhood and treat the diners to a song. Talented young singers still perform between table service at Victor's*

◀ **Philadelphia Museum of Art:** *Designed by Julian Abele, the museum houses one of the world's finest collections. Its interior boasts a grand stone staircase, with a bronze figure of Diana the Huntress by Augustus Saint-Gaudens. The museum sponsors evening programs that integrate the performing arts and gourmet meals, among other things.*

◄ **Rodin Museum:**
Philadelphia's Rodin Museum boasts a collection of Auguste Rodin sculptures to rival those of the Paris museum that is also devoted to his work. Theater magnate Jules E. Mastbaum began the collection in 1923 and commissioned architects Jacque Greber and Paul Cret to design the museum and garden. Two versions of The Thinker can be found here, one of them a small statue at the pinnacle of his tragic frieze, The Gates of Hell. The Burghers of Calais, Eternal Springtime, and The Apotheosis of Victor Hugo are also among the museum's 124 pieces.

▲ **Eastern State Penitentiary:** *The most expensive building in early nineteenth-century America was not the U.S. Capitol in Washington, D.C., but Eastern State Penitentiary in Philadelphia. This was a Quaker experiment inspired by the hope that prisoners would meditate in solitude and emerge repentant. The cheerless fortress walls were meant to show "the misery which awaits the unhappy beings who enter." Celebrity inmates have included Al Capone and Willie Sutton. Willie escaped with other inmates through a long underground tunnel, but was captured only a few minutes after he emerged. The penitentiary is now a popular tourist attraction.*

▲ **Marian Anderson House:** *This house at 732 Martin Street in South Philadelphia is remarkable not for its architecture, but for its place in the life of the great contralto Marian Anderson. She grew up in the city and maintained this as her residence from 1924 to 1990. Marian Anderson often faced racist slights as she sang around the nation. She was prohibited from performing in Constitutional Hall in Washington, which was controlled by the Daughters of the American Revolution. However, her open-air Easter concert on the steps of the Lincoln Memorial in 1939 brought her talents to millions of radio listeners, and the disgraceful treatment came to full public attention.*

▲ **Franklin Institute:**
Founded in 1824 to promote
scientific study and inventions,
the Franklin Institute moved
into this grand building in
1934. Before the rear wall
was closed up, the 101-foot-
long Baldwin 60000, the
largest steam locomotive ever
made, was hauled on
temporary tracks to its place
of honor. The Franklin
Institute established the
nation's first weather bureau
and offered the first formal
course in architecture.
Modern visitors can enjoy the
IMAX theater and, on their
way, climb through a two-
story human heart.

▶ **Logan Circle
Fountain:** One of the
original squares planned by
William Penn as a park,
Logan Square was once
pasture land and a graveyard,
and also hosted an occasional
hanging, like William Gross's in
1823. However, when the
twentieth-century parkway
was laid out between City
Hall and the Museum of Art,
Logan Square instead
became a traffic circle.
Alexander Sterling Calder, son
of the sculptor of all the
statues on City Hall and
father of the mobile designer,
Sandy Calder, sculpted the
graceful allegorical figures
around the Swann Memorial
Fountain. They represent the
Delaware, Schuylkill, and
Wissahickon rivers.

▲ **Four Seasons:** *The elegant Fountain Restaurant at the Four Seasons vies with Le Bec-Fin as the spot for Philadelphia's finest dining. Its windows look out on Logan Circle, a very romantic view to accompany a superb dining experience.*

▲ **Mutter Museum:** *Entering the Mutter Museum on Twenty-Second Street takes visitors into a world that predates the discovery of the modern medicines now taken for granted. Stark anatomical exhibits include the original Siamese twins and an inside look at the intrigue surrounding the nation's sickest presidents. This window into the nineteenth-century medical world presents courageous patients and the devoted doctors who so often were not able to cure them.*

▶ **Love Sculpture:** *Robert Indiana (née Clark) once confessed to a group of Philadelphia art students that he was "not a sculptor by any means. It was one of my worst subjects at school." Yet in his obsession with word images, he created one of the most plagiarized pieces of artwork in the country. Originally loaned to the city to celebrate the nation's Bicentennial in 1976, the sculpture has been there ever since.*

▶ **Wilma Theater:**
This playhouse grew out a feminist collective in 1973; the name "Wilma" derived from a fictitious feminine persona for William Shakespeare. Under the brilliant leadership of Czechoslovakians Blanka and Jiri Zizka, it aims for explosive theater that reflects the complexities of contemporary life.

▶ **Walnut Street Theatre:** *The oldest English theater in continuous use stands on the corner of Ninth and Walnut Streets in Philadelphia. Built in 1809, it has played host to Sarah Benhardt, George M. Cohan, Claudette Colbert, Houdini, Helen Hayes, Groucho Marx, and Katherine Hepburn. Its subscription audience is the largest of any regional theater company in the world.*

◀ **Settlement Music School:** *Following a modest start as a service center for new immigrants, this organization has blossomed into America's largest community-based arts school, with six branches. The students who paid a nickel in 1908 for piano lessons taught by two volunteers could not have foreseen that Settlement would someday produce distinguished graduates like Andre Watts, one of the most sought-after concert pianists in the world.*

▶ **Academy of Vocal Arts:** *Founded when the United States was in the grip of the Great Depression in 1933, the Academy of Vocal Arts offered talented singers tuition-free training. Dedicated teachers and artists from the world of opera still provide high quality vocal and theatrical education to those admitted into this highly competitive academy for emerging professionals, and their services are still tuition-free.*

▲ **Academy of Music:**
"America's La Scala," the
Italianate-Revival Academy
of Music is the longest
continuously operating
music hall in the country.
Built in 1851 for "Operas in
English and Italian, concerts,
drama, pantomime and
French Vaudeville," it also
hosted the world's first indoor
football game in 1889. In
order to provide the best
acoustics, a thirty-foot

concave dome in the ceiling
above the grand Victorian
chandelier matches a thirty-
foot well in the basement.
The floorboards under the
orchestra seats were laid
loosely enough to vibrate in
the dancing column of air.
American opera premieres
here have included Il
Trovatore, Faust, and The
Flying Dutchman.

▶ **Franklin Memorial:**
James Earle Fraser's imposing
sculpture at the entrance to
the Franklin Institute is the
official national monument
for Benjamin Franklin. Made
from thirty tons of seravezza
marble, the statue rests on a
Portuguese marble base. The
artist intended to portray
Franklin as "a massive figure,
tranquil in body, with latent
power in his hands, but with
an inquisitive expression in

the movement of his head
and the alertness of his eyes,
ready to turn the full force of
his keen mind on any
problem that concerned him."
It is a fitting tribute to one of
the United States' most
important figures.

▲ **Cliveden:**

Benjamin Chew, Penn family lawyer and eventually Pennsylvania Chief Justice, built this home near Germantown. With its roof topped by five imported urns, it is considered one of the finest country-Palladian houses in America. British troops were quartered at Cliveden during Washington's unsuccessful attack at the Battle of Germantown.

▶ **Johnson House:**

This 1768 stone house at 6306 Germantown Avenue is one of America's best-preserved Underground Railroad sites. Now a private, non-profit organization, it conducts special house tours showing visitors the Johnson family's hiding places for runaway slaves. Abolitionist leaders William Still and Harriet Tubman also used the house as a meeting place.

◀ **Stenton:** *James Logan built his "plain cheap farmer's stone house" along the Germantown Pike in 1730. Logan, reputed inventor of the covered wagon, is the namesake of Logan Circle. His simple innovation meant that the German farmers could haul produce into town and sleep in their wagons overnight. Adroit administrator for William Penn's colony and master of a dozen languages, Logan also owned the largest library in the colonies and became an advisor for Franklin's lending library. Located at 4601 North Eighteenth Street, this handsome colonial house welcomes the public.*

▲ **Deshler-Morris House:** *Built as a residence for merchant David Deshler, the house served triple duty. British commander William Howe used it in October 1777 as his headquarters during the Battle of Germantown. Later, President Washington retreated from Philadelphia's yellow fever epidemics in 1793 and 1794, making this the first "Summer White House." Although the president paid over $30 a month in rent, he was charged an extra $2.50 by the owner for "Cleaning my house and putting it in the same condition..." after he vacated it.*

◀ **Allen's Lane Station:** *This is one of the many picturesque stations along the suburban lines that connect neighborhoods like Mount Airy and Chestnut Hill to Center City Philadelphia. Seen in earlier decades as outmoded, they are now prized and protected by the residents of these communities as a touch of grace in a technological world.*

▲ **Chestnut Hill:** *Once a pre-Revolutionary village of gristmills and way houses, Chestnut Hill's residents were full of such "intense wickedness" that their village had no churches. Now beautiful masonry churches of every kind line its heights. Residents stroll Germantown Avenue for antiques, gift shops, hobby and craft stores, books, flowers, jewelry, and restaurants, both gourmet and casual. Three centuries of growth and restoration have resulted in an architecturally rich neighborhood with its own unique charm.*

▶ **Manayunk Bridge:** *The Lenape Indians called this part of the Schuylkill River "our place for drinking." Construction of a dam, with an adjacent canal and lock system, made Manayunk a major manufacturing center of the nineteenth century. In 1854, it was integrated into Philadelphia, its steep hills and crooked narrow streets a foil to the flat, open grid pattern of Center City. Following a long industrial decline, Manayunk's residents gentrified their main street and it now boasts upscale shops and restaurants, as well as neighborhood pubs, and it is ringed by row houses on the surrounding hills.*

Waterfront and South Philadelphia

Several great suspension bridges span the Delaware River, but the most popular remains the Depression-era WPA project—the big, blue Benjamin Franklin Bridge, brightened at night by dancing lights. Just south of it, on both banks of the Delaware, are the city's most visited riverfront attractions. The Camden side boasts the beautiful Campbell's Field, with its outfield nestled against the bridge, the Adventure Aquarium, where the public can swim with the fishes, and the most decorated of American battleships, the retired U.S.S. *New Jersey*.

On the Philadelphia riverbank, visitors can enjoy the Seaport Museum, visit the *Olympia*, the flagship of the nineteenth-century U.S. fleet, and dine on board the *Moshulu*, the world's largest sailing ship turned floating restaurant. South Street starts close to the berth of the *Moshulu* and slices west across the city, offering three centuries of Bohemian Philadelphia.

Further south of South Street, visitors can see scenes that were already familiar before they appeared in the *Rocky* films—the Italian Market and the great cheese steak standoff, down by Geno's and Pat's. The close-knit Italian neighborhood boasts many of the city's most prominent clubs whose performers dress up in feathers and paint for the famous Mummers Parade on New Year's Day. Famous sons of South Philadelphia have included Frankie Avalon, Bobby Rydell, James Darren and tenor Mario Lanza.

▶ **Benjamin Franklin Bridge:** *Dedicated on July 1, 1926, the Benjamin Franklin Bridge was then the world's longest suspension bridge. French architect Paul Cret designed the massive stone towers and, not leaving anything to chance, the bridge also has a massive girder system along with its oversized suspension cables—like wearing a belt and suspenders. Different sets of lights brighten the bridge at night, including spotlights that illuminate the inverted arch of the cable and blink as the Hi-Speed Line cars cross the bridge.*

◀ **South Street:**
William Penn named the
southernmost street of his
city Cedar, and even in the
eighteenth century it was the
Bohemian part of town. The
Quakers insisted that theater
and dance was "a waste of
God's time," so all the
theaters were erected on the
south side of the street,
outside the city limits. With
recently added sparkle from
the artworks of Isaiah Zagar,
South Street is still a great
place to eat, shop, and
people-watch.

▲ **Geno's:** Just south of
the Italian Market, Pat's and
Geno's still square off twenty-
four hours a day, competing
over the famous Philadelphia
cheese steak. Who invented
it? Who has the best? It is a
ritual for politicians of every
stripe to down one of these
famous sandwiches, while
avoiding stains on their ties.

▲▲ Adventure Aquarium:
This popular site on the Camden side of the Delaware River features a two-story exhibit with an underwater shark tunnel. Visitors find themselves surrounded by the predatory eyes of twenty sharks and 850 other sea creatures as they walk through. They can even arrange to hop in the water and swim with the sharks, presumably after feeding time. Its Jules Verne Gallery contains exotic sea dragons, giant spider crabs, and the giant Pacific octopus.

▲ Citizens Bank Park:
The Philadelphia skyline, a genuine grass field, and a melange of interesting eateries, not to mention the Phillie Phanatic, make Citizens Bank Park baseball stadium a fun place. The city's new basketball arena, and the football stadium are all within walking distance of one another.

▶ Campbell's Field:
Built in 2001 to help revitalize Camden City's waterfront, this minor league baseball stadium is named for the great cannery, which is still headquartered in the city, Campbell Soup Co. Fans of the Camden Riversharks have one of the best views of the Philadelphia skyline from the left field wall. The outfield reaches almost to the base of the Franklin Bridge, though there is no risk that a home run will pick off the windshield of a passing motorist.

◀ **Moshulu and Olympia:** *Philadelphia is no longer the world's largest freshwater port, but it remains one of the prime locations for historic ships. The world's largest sailing ship, the iron clad clipper* Moshulu, *floats at Penn's Landing in Philadelphia and is now an upscale restaurant serving food with a South Seas flair, reminiscent of the ship's trade routes. Directly in Moshulu's sights is the shorter but more pugnacious steam cruiser U.S.S. Olympia. The oldest steel-hulled American warship afloat, Olympia was the flagship of the U.S. fleet in the late nineteenth century, and also served during World War I.*

▲ **Battleship New Jersey:** *The U.S.S. New Jersey was launched at Philadelphia Naval Shipyard in 1942 and soon saw action in World War II. One of the largest battleships of the American fleet, she was successively refitted for the Korean War and for service off the coast of Vietnam. Battleship New Jersey remained in service until 1991, and was finally returned in retirement to the navy yard, which by then was also retired. Now one of the visitor attractions on the Camden waterfront, she is again in the river of her birth.*

▶ **Samuel S. Fleisher Art Memorial:** *Located in South Philadelphia at 719 Catharine Street, the Fleisher Art Memorial is the nation's largest tuition-free art school. Fleisher connected a small school building to the neighboring Romanesque-Revival church, which had been designed by architect Frank Furness. His own collection of medieval religious art is exhibited in the historic sanctuary, the place he called a "playground for the soul." The school and gallery represent one of many treasures Philadelphia's eccentric and generous philanthropists have bequeathed to the city.*

Circling the City

The outer ring surrounding Philadelphia is an eclectic mix of brilliant architecture, Revolutionary monuments, bucolic towns, unique cultures, picturesque foliage, artists' colonies, and a treasure trove of charming sites. The arc north of Philadelphia connects two significant sites of General Washington's wartime leadership: Washington Crossing State Park on the Delaware, where the commander's bold move surprised the Hessian troops in Trenton, and Valley Forge, where his reduced army improved their military skills for battles yet to come. This region is rich with attractions: architectural wonders like the Frank Lloyd Wright synagogue in Elkins Park and the quirky buildings of Henry Chapman Mercer. Highlights along the Delaware include charming colonial inns and riverside restaurants, reaching to the artists' enclave at New Hope.

A drive directly west of the city, easier now that the Conestoga wagon trails are highways, takes visitors along the "main line," the wealthy world of *The Philadelphia Story*, and out to the lands of Amish farmers in Lancaster County. Curving south around Philadelphia brings visitors to Chadds Ford where they can view the paintings of Andrew Wyeth, whose home is nearby, at the Brandywine River Museum. Also close is La Fayette's stone house in Brandywine Battlefield State Park. These rolling hills are not far from Dupont country and Pierre S. Du Pont's amazing Longwood Gardens.

▶ **Brandywine River Museum:** *Internationally known for its signature collection of works by three generations of the Wyeth family, the Brandywine River Museum occupies a nineteenth-century gristmill next to the Brandywine River. The modern addition to the museum rises naturally from the wildflower gardens and river walks. Visitors to the Brandywine often take time to visit one of the other nearby museums and gardens, many of them connected to the Dupont family.*

◀ **Pennsbury Manor:** *Although William Penn designed the city of brotherly love, he established his own 8,000-acre estate twenty-six miles up river, preferring the country life: "for there we see the Works of God; but in Cities little else but the Works of Men." His grandson Richard demolished the building shortly before the Revolutionary War, and the current Pennsbury Manor was built in the 1930s. Though not a perfect replica, this beautiful site still evokes old Pennsylvania.*

▲ **Fonthill:** *One of Philadelphia's great eccentrics, Henry Chapman Mercer, was fascinated with tools and early crafts. His enthusiasms drove him to establish the highly regarded Moravian Pottery and Tile Works. By 1910, he had built an extravagant, castle-like forty-four-room mansion to match the plaster-of-Paris model he had aleady made. He called Fonthill his "concrete castle for the New World."*

▶ **Washington Crossing:** *Emanuel Leutze's painting,* Washington Crossing the Delaware, *turned the bold maneuver of George Washington into an American myth. After losing New York, Washington moved south to stretch General Howe's army across New Jersey, with their outposts out of New York's range. Washington's forces slipped across the icy river in large, ore-carrying Durham boats, and caught the Hessian soldiers sleeping off their Christmas celebrations.*

New Hope: *The New Hope and Ivyland Railroad takes passengers aboard 1920s vintage cars along the same route filmed in the 1914 movie* Perils of Pauline, *and is just one of the dozens of attractions in this charming artists' village on the banks of the upper Delaware River. Weekends find its many gourmet restaurants packed, as well as the popular Bucks County Playhouse. Oscar Hammerstein, Pearl S. Buck, and James Michener have all resided nearby.*

▲ **Beth Shalom Synagogue:** *Frank Lloyd Wright designed this religious building in the shape of a gigantic glass pyramid for Beth Sholom Synagogue in Elkins Park, north of Philadelphia. An inspiring religious space, it is brilliantly illuminated due to its translucent roof. Symbols of the Menorah are arrayed along the spines of the pyramid.*

◄▲ **Valley Forge:**

After their defeat by the British at the Battle of Brandywine, Washington's remaining army of 7,000 men reached a knoll above the Schuylkill River at Valley Forge in late December, 1777. Washington and his officers commandeered local houses, paying a fee for the season, and the president made his own headquarters at Isaac Potts' fieldstone house (left). The soldiers managed to build a total of 2,000 log huts to help them survive the winter cold. Although the white covered bridge above was not erected until 1865, it adds a touch of grace to the rolling parklands.

TO THE OFFICERS AND PRIVATE SOLDIERS
OF THE CONTINENTAL ARMY
DECEMBER 19, 1777   JUNE 19, 1778

◀ **National Memorial Arch:** *Erected on June 25, 1910, this striking granite and bronze decorated monument marks the entrance of the Continental Army into the Valley Forge encampment. Designed by the University of Pennsylvania professor Paul Philippe Cret, it is built in the style of the Triumphal Arch of Titus in Rome, which celebrated the capture of Jerusalem by the emperors Vespasian and Titus in AD 70. The south elevation includes an inscription from Washington at Valley Forge, dated February 16, 1778: "Naked and starving as they are we cannot enough admire incomparable patience and fidelity of the soldiery."*

▶ **Amish Country:** *Fifty miles west of Philadelphia, on the fertile rolling hills of Lancaster County, remnants of pacifist religious sects who followed Penn to his colony, still cling to a lifestyle predating the twentieth century. The Amish in particular maintain their connection to God's earth, using windmills to power their pumps and mules to pull their plows. Sadly, increased tourism and commercial encroachments, partially attributable to the hit movie Witness, now threaten their way of life.*

▲ **Devon Train Depot:** *Following the example of William Penn who founded Philadelphia and then moved to the suburbs, many of the wealthy industrialists and railroad magnates of Philadelphia moved out of the city in the late nineteenth century to build their mansions in the western suburbs. The main suburban line of the railroad connected each of these communities and whisked these men from the Main Line to their offices in Center City.*

◀ **Swarthmore
College:** *Founded in 1860
by liberal Hicksite Quakers
including Lucretia Mott, a
leading champion of abolition
and women's rights, the
college was planned as a
co-educational experience
"equal to that of the best
institutions of learning in our
country." Their vision has
indeed been realized in this,
the top-ranked private college
in America. Its tradition of
excellence also includes a
tradition of community
service, to match the ideal of
the Religious Society of
Friends.*

 **Brandywine Battlefield:** *The Battle of Brandywine might have given Washington's army their first major victory were it not for a single spy. Instead, his defeated army was reduced from 15,000 to 7,000 stalwarts who spent the winter of 1777–78 at Valley Forge. The Marquis de LaFayette first saw military action as Washington's aide at Brandywine. He was quartered in Gideon Gilpin's house, which was plundered by the British army after the battle. His losses included "10 milch cows, 28 swine, 230 bushels of wheat, a history book, and 1 gun."*

▲▶ Longwood Gardens: *A magnificent horticultural showplace covering over 1,000 acres of gardens, woodlands, greenhouses, and illuminated fountains, the Longwood Gardens feature 11,000 types of flowers, plants, and trees. Longwood also hosts 800 events each year, from concerts to fireworks, drawing hundreds of thousands of visitors.*

Index

Map of Philadelphia

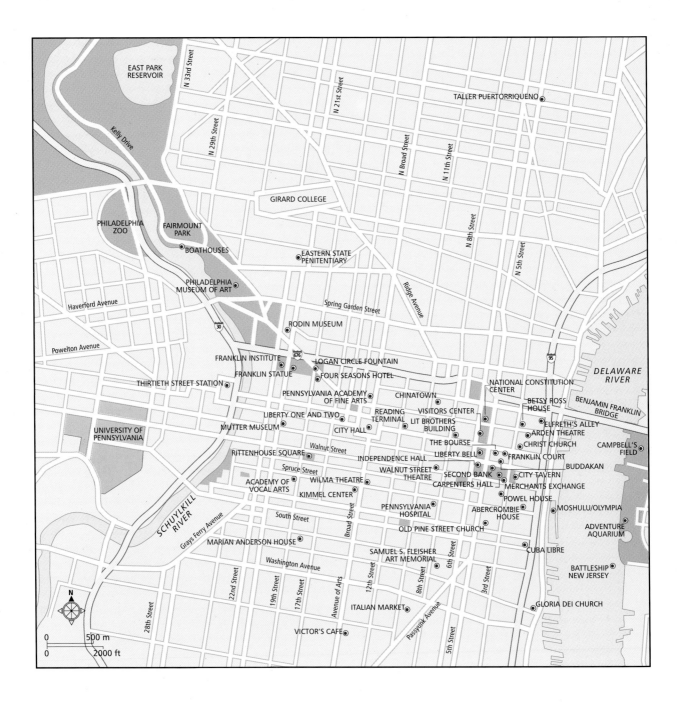